This book is dedicated to all the wild animals that have
blessed me with beautiful windows into their lives.

Baby Animals
Playing

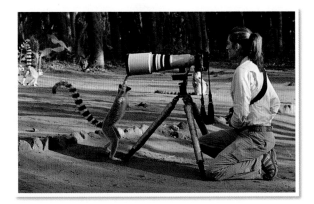

SUZI ESZTERHAS

Owlkids Books

Baby animals love to play. Playing helps their bodies grow and gives them a chance to practice the skills they need to survive. And it's fun! Let's see what these wild animal babies are doing today.

This lion cub has found a toy! She uses her strong teeth and paws to attack her stick.

Baby lemurs like climbing trees. Gripping the branches makes their hands and fingers stronger. Hang on tight, little lemur!

Raccoon kits perch high in the treetops. It's a safe place to hang out while Mom looks for food below.

Dad's big belly is soft and bouncy. After a short rest, it will be the perfect place for a baby gorilla to play.

A giraffe calf races through the grass. She will need to be quick to get away from predators. Go, giraffe, go!

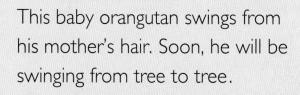

This baby orangutan swings from his mother's hair. Soon, he will be swinging from tree to tree.

A bison calf butts heads with her mom. She is playing now, but one day this is how she will protect herself in the wild.

A chimpanzee tumbles across the rainforest floor. He rolls and flips as he explores his home.

These cheetah brothers wrestle each other. They are learning how to hunt and fight other animals.

Brown bear cubs play by the river. They already know how to swim. Soon, Mom will teach them how to fish for salmon.

Jackal pups play with a ball of elephant poop.
They are learning to work together as a team.

Sometimes the pups fight over the ball.
Each one wants a turn to play!

3-2-1... Blast off! A baby dolphin uses his tail to launch himself out of the water like a rocket.

Playing and learning is hard work. A sleepy capybara curls up on Mom's back. It's nap time!

This baby chimpanzee found a toy. I watched her carry her special stick around for days.

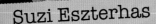
Suzi Eszterhas

This cheetah cub made me laugh when she jumped on Mom's head. She stayed there for a while, and Mom was patient the whole time.

Hi, I'm Suzi!

I travel all over the world taking pictures of animals. I also help animal conservationists by telling their stories and helping to raise money for their causes. When I'm not snapping photos, I like to talk to people about how they can help wild animals. I think it's important for kids to connect with animals and nature. You can do this by looking at photos, reading books, or just by going outside and playing in nature like these baby animals do!

Normally, I don't touch or hold wild baby animals. But on this day, I was working with a group of biologists in Canada. While they were helping the mother polar bear, they asked me to hold the cub. His fur was so soft!

This lemur in Madagascar wanted to play with my camera. He walked right up to me, peeked in my lens, and hung on with his little hand.

Feet make great toys! I loved watching this brown bear cub roll around and play with his huge foot.

Sometimes baby animals get scared when they are playing. This baby lemur got frightened while climbing high in a tree. But when he grows up, he will be a fearless climber.

Newborn babies, like these jackal pups, sleep a lot. And they like to snuggle with their siblings. I spent months watching this jackal family. Every day I took pictures of the pups as they grew.

Consultant: Chris Earley, Interpretive Biologist, University of Guelph Arboretum

Owlkids Books acknowledges the financial support of the Canada Council for the Arts, the Ontario Arts Council, the Government of Canada through the Canada Book Fund (CBF) and the Government of Ontario through the Ontario Media Development Corporation's Book Initiative for our publishing activities.

Published in Canada by
Owlkids Books Inc.
10 Lower Spadina Avenue
Toronto, ON M5V 2Z2

Published in the United States by
Owlkids Books Inc.
1700 Fourth Street
Berkeley, CA 94710

Library and Archives Canada Cataloguing in Publication

Eszterhas, Suzi, author, photographer
    Baby animals playing / words and photos by Suzi Eszterhas.

(Baby animals)
ISBN 978-1-77147-297-5 (hardcover)

    1. Play behavior in animals--Pictorial works--Juvenile literature. 2. Animals--Infancy--Pictorial works--Juvenile literature. I. Title.

QL763.5.E89 2017   j591.56'3   C2017-900008-X

Library of Congress Control Number: 2016962519

Edited by: Jackie Farquhar
Designed by: Danielle Arbour

Manufactured in Dongguan, China, in April 2017, by Toppan Leefung Packaging & Printing (Dongguan) Co., Ltd.
Job #BAYDC41

A   B   C   D   E   F

Publisher of Chirp, chickaDEE and OWL
www.owlkidsbooks.com

Owlkids Books is a division of